Roman Britain: A Very Short Introduction

VERY SHORT INTRODUCTIONS are for anyone wanting a stimulating and accessible way in to a new subject. They are written by experts, and have been published in more than 25 languages worldwide.

The series began in 1995, and now represents a wide variety of topics in history, philosophy, religion, science, and the humanities. Over the next few years it will grow to a library of around 200 volumes – a Very Short Introduction to everything from ancient Egypt and Indian philosophy to conceptual art and cosmology.

Very Short Introductions available now:

Available soon:

For more information visit our web site

www.oup.co.uk/vsi

Peter Salway

ROMAN BRITAIN

A Very Short Introduction

OXFORD
UNIVERSITY PRESS

OXFORD
UNIVERSITY PRESS

Great Clarendon Street, Oxford ox2 6dp

Oxford University Press is a department of the University of Oxford.
It furthers the University's objective of excellence in research, scholarship,
and education by publishing worldwide in

Oxford New York

Auckland Bangkok Buenos Aires Cape Town Chennai
Dar es Salaam Delhi Hong Kong Istanbul Karachi Kolkata
Kuala Lumpur Madrid Melbourne Mexico City Mumbai Nairobi
São Paulo Shanghai Taipei Tokyo Toronto

Oxford is a registered trade mark of Oxford University Press
in the UK and in certain other countries

Published in the United States
by Oxford University Press Inc., New York

Text © Peter Salway 1984

The moral rights of the author have been asserted

Database right Oxford University Press (maker)

Text first published in *The Oxford Illustrated History of Britain* 1984
First published as a Very Short Introduction 2000

British Library Cataloguing in Publication Data

Data available

Library of Congress Cataloging in Publication Data

Data available

ISBN-13: 978-0-19-285404-9

ISBN-10: 0-19-285404-6

5 7 9 10 8 6

Typeset by RefineCatch Ltd, Bungay, Suffolk
Printed in Great Britain by
Ashford Colour Press Ltd, Gosport, Hamshire

Contents

List of Illustrations

The publisher and the author apologize for any errors or omissions in the above list. If contacted they will be pleased to rectify these at the earliest opportunity.

List of Maps

Chapter 1
The Beginnings of British History

In Roman times Britain had as many people as at its peak in the Middle Ages. For four centuries it was an integral part of a single political system that stretched from Turkey to Portugal and from the Red Sea to the Tyne and beyond. Its involvement with Rome started before the Conquest launched by Claudius in AD 43, and it continued to be a part of the Roman world for some time after the final break with Roman rule. We are dealing with a full half-millennium of the history of Britain.

The origins of later Britain go back beyond the Roman period. Aspects of the society the Romans found in Britain were beginning to emerge in the Neolithic and Early Bronze Ages. At the time of the Roman Conquest, the culture of Britain had something like fifteen hundred to two thousand years of development behind it – although the prehistorians are greatly divided on the details. By the end of the Pre-Roman Iron Age, society had evolved forms of organization closely similar to those encountered by the Romans elsewhere in north-western Europe, and had adopted versions of the culture and language we loosely call 'Celtic'. Outside the imperial frontiers in Britain these continued largely unchanged; inside, the Celtic substratum persisted, assimilated and adapted by Rome in ways not in general closely paralleled by modern colonial empires.

Why, then, does 'history' neither start in Britain long before the

Romans, nor consign Roman Britain, as some modern writers would have us do, to 'prehistory'? The answer lies in the real distinction between the Roman period and what went before. There is *some* truth in the assertion that the study of Roman Britain is prehistory, in the sense that we have to lean very heavily on archaeology – and this is also true of the early Anglo-Saxon period. However, our sources for Britain are by no means solely archaeological, and the interpretation of the material remains themselves cannot be divorced from the study of the written sources. It is true that the quantity of contemporary or near-contemporary literary evidence is not great in comparison with later periods but there is enough to be significant. Moreover, we have the very considerable remains of the once- huge routine output of a literate society – and in a form not subject to the inevitable corruptions of the Greek and Latin literary texts, which have largely survived only by being copied and re-copied by hand down the centuries. Actual examples of writing found in Britain, mostly as inscriptions on stone but some in other forms, constitute a major primary source for the Romano-British period. They include trade marks on manufactured goods; a small but growing number of personal letters and other documents in a variety of materials discovered in excavations; even graffiti – the everyday writing and reading matter of ordinary people. Nor can we ignore the specialized and difficult but rewarding study of Roman coinage, which played a peculiarly important part in the politics and economics of the Roman world. Not only was the currency itself manipulated by government as money, but also the wording and images upon the coins were exploited as a powerful medium for mass propaganda with all the persistence of a regularly screened television commercial in our own time. The ability to read was, admittedly, very much commoner in the towns than in the Romano-British countryside but it was compulsory in the army and essential in many other walks of life. It was certainly not, as in other ages, restricted to a small or specialized class.

The critical difference between Roman Britain and what went before is that its society was literate, perhaps more literate than at any other time

1. A Romano-British lady? A mosaic floor laid in the middle of the fourth century in the bath-house of a villa at Thenford, Northamptonshire: probably the goddess Diana, but possibly a portrait

until the end of the Middle Ages. Alongside and allied to this is the fact that it was a world dominated by the rule of law, which closely regulated the relations between the individual and the State and between one man and another, however corruptly or inefficiently it might often have been administered. As a society that became more and more dominated by regulations and procedures contained in official documents, the contrast between Roman Britain and Britain as it was at the end of the Pre-Roman Iron Age is startling. Then, even at the top of the social scale where the import of Roman luxury goods was a notable feature, writing was totally absent except on the splendid but limited coinage – and even on that the language employed was almost universally Latin and the moneyers themselves often Roman.

3

Once Julius Caesar's expeditions of 55 and 54 BC had pointed the way, it was more or less inevitable that Rome would try her hand at conquest. Romans did not acknowledge any limit on their right to expand their rule: indeed, they saw it as a divine mission. From Caesar onwards, Britain occupied a particular and significant place in the Roman consciousness. The Roman period is a turning-point, not so much in the underlying story of man's settlement of the land of Britain but in the country's emergence from prehistory into history.

The Physical Landscape

The character of the physical geography of a country has a great effect on how people live, and Britain is no exception. Its outstanding permanent characteristic is the broad division between 'highland' and 'lowland' – in rough terms, between the north and west of mainland Britain and the south and east – but it is a distinction which can be overdone in historical analysis. Moreover, the inhabitants of Britain have shown a considerable capacity to adapt the landscape, sometimes intentionally, often in pursuit of some other end such as fuel. There have also been important fluctuations in the physical conditions, especially in the relative level of land and sea, with considerable effects on the coastline and inland on the pattern and level of rivers. To what extent the causes were climatic or a matter of movements in the geology is uncertain. In general, such evidence as we have for the Roman period suggests that the climate was broadly similar to present-day Britain's. A period of relatively high sea level was succeeded by a 'marine regression', opening up new lands for exploitation. In the third century the onset of rather wetter climatic conditions seems to be revealed by evidence of flooding in many parts of Europe, with serious problems for low-lying land, rivers, and harbours. So it would seem that climatic conditions were by no means constant throughout the period.

The once-popular belief that Britain was largely covered with forest until cleared by the Anglo-Saxons is now discredited. By the Roman

Conquest, although there was still a great deal of natural forest, the population had already grown to something of the order it reached under the Romans, two or three times greater than during the reign of William the Conqueror (1066–87). The proportion of forest to open, settled landscape had dropped to the level of the Later Middle Ages. From the latter part of the second millennium BC what was to become the classic Iron Age pattern was starting to take shape: hillforts, isolated farms or groups of farms sometimes amounting to villages (often surrounded by small enclosures), larger expanses of permanent fields, woodland, and great open stretches of pasture. In the last 750 years before Caesar, Britain adopted many of the characteristics of the successive phases of the Continental Iron Age, though often with insular variations. This has led to unresolved debate among the prehistorians as to whether the changes that succeeded one another primarily reflect actual invasions on a substantial scale, the arrival of relatively small numbers of influential or conquering newcomers (as later the Normans), or the exchange of ideas through travel and trade. But whatever the mechanism, Britain had reached the point by Caesar's time where, as he himself says, the tribes he met in the parts he penetrated – the south and east – were very similar to those he encountered in Gaul. Beyond these, archaeology reveals that there were some less advanced peoples, but all of them seem to have shared the same British version of the Celtic language and a broadly similar culture.

Social Organization

There is some reason to think that the tribal system we find in Britain in Claudian times was not fully developed in Caesar's, and there are other important changes in the period between the Roman invasions which we shall examine later (see page 10). In southern Gaul, the native tribes had largely passed from rule by kings to elective magistracies and tribal councils, but in northern Gaul kingship was still common when Caesar arrived. In Britain it was to remain so down to Claudius, though there are some signs of joint or divided rule by pairs of kings. Society divided broadly into a warrior aristocracy and a largely agricultural commons. The priests, the druids, were a third group whose position and function are debated, though for Britain the balance of the evidence is still against the popular notion of their having a prominent political role. The Celts were characterized by quarrelsomeness, both within the tribe and in their indulgence in inter-tribal warfare. Only on rare occasions, in the face of great danger, would Celtic tribes combine to choose a single leader; though in Gaul at least there was some tradition of periodic gatherings of prominent men from various tribes. There was little or no 'national' sentiment.

By Caesar's day, close relationships had been established between southern Britain and northern Gaul. The pattern of archaeological finds reveals two main groups of routes by which goods and people travelled between the two countries. The most important at this time was between Brittany and Lower Normandy (in ancient times known collectively as Armorica) and south-west Britain, particularly through a port at Hengistbury Head in Dorset. The other routes were from Upper Normandy and the Low Countries, the lands between the mouths of the Seine and Rhine, to southern and eastern England. Caesar moreover reports that 'within living memory' a Gallic ruler had exercised power in Britain as well as his own homeland, and he was not only to find British contingents fighting alongside his Gallic enemies but to be thwarted by fugitives seeking refuge from Rome with friends or kin across the Channel.

The Expansion of Rome

To understand why Caesar was in Gaul and what may have prompted his campaigns in Britain we need to look briefly at the condition of Rome at this time. Rome's expansion in the third and second centuries BC from being an Italian city state to the greatest power in the Mediterranean had been under her traditional form of government. This was theoretically democratic, with assemblies of the people and annually elected magistrates, but in practice public office was held century after century by a relatively small number of aristocratic families. The senate, notionally an advisory body, came to have a dominant role, being composed of magistrates and all those who had previously been elected to the qualifying magistracies. The highest offices, the two annual consulships, were almost exclusively held by an even smaller group within the senatorial class, and its families possessed special prestige. Religious and social attitudes, closely intertwined, placed a very high value on veneration of the family ancestors and the preservation of family honour. It was a characteristic of the classical world that a man's reputation – what his peers thought of him – was of the highest importance. At Rome, the individual aristocrat was under constant pressure, both of family duty and personal ambition, to emulate his forebears by pursuing a public career and by striving for the highest office.

Reputation was won by success primarily in two fields: the law and the army. A senatorial career normally included posts in both areas. Of the two, proven military prowess won the greater prestige. Holding certain senior offices, even below the consulship, brought with it eligibility to command armies and govern provinces abroad. Caesar's contemporary, the orator, politician, and moralist Cicero, states categorically what conferred the greatest personal status: there was more glory to be won by extending the empire than by administering it.

In the ancient world, wars of conquest usually showed a handsome profit for the victor. The immense wealth brought into Rome by her conquests and the opportunities and temptations offered by her Mediterranean empire put intolerable strains on the political and social system that had been adequate for a small Italian state. By the middle of the first century BC, the Roman Republic was falling apart. The old conventions within the governing class could not cope. Ambition to join the select few at the top had been replaced by an inability to tolerate even equals in power and fame.

Part of the visible prestige of a great Roman aristocrat had long been the number of people dependent upon him. Indeed, whole communities could regard themselves as among his 'clients'. Such 'patronage' was a feature of society that was to be of great importance to provinces such as Britain, otherwise far from the centre of power. By the first century BC, the old citizen armies, raised for a specific war, had been replaced by professionals. The senate made the fatal mistake of allowing these new soldiers to become dependent upon their own generals rather than the State for the rewards of service, particularly the all-important provision on retirement. The conditions for recurrent civil war were now all present and the Republic effectively doomed. Attitudes, practices, and social relationships had been set up that were to haunt Rome for the rest of her history. For Britain, it was not only the great events of the subsequent history of the empire that directly affected her destiny, but also the extraordinary success the Romans had in transmitting their values to the populations they absorbed – particularly to the native ruling classes. Indeed, the creation of a common upper-class culture, critical to the successful working of the empire itself, was in many ways also central in its downfall. The story of Britain in Roman times reflects this fundamental pattern.

Caesar's British Campaigns, 55 and 54 BC

Julius Caesar's conquest of Gaul must be looked at in the context of the struggle for power in the closing years of the Republic. We shall probably never know exactly why he launched his two expeditions to Britain in 55 and 54 BC, nor whether he intended conquest – though there is a possible parallel in his punitive foray across the Rhine into Germany. More important were the consequences for the future. In immediate military terms the results were modest, though we do not hear of Britons fighting in Gaul again. Because of the explosive state of Gaul, Caesar was prevented from following up his victories and from taking advantage of the surrender of the temporary confederation of the British tribes. Indeed, a Roman historian writing in the next century even represented a British leader as claiming the 'repulse' of Caesar by the ancestors of his listeners.

Caesar's British enterprise made a lasting impression on Rome, however. Britain was a remote, almost fabled island across the 'Ocean', a fearsome sea to Romans as yet unaccustomed to the tidal conditions outside the Mediterranean. Britain was beyond the known world. In two brief campaigns Caesar had put Britain on the Roman map. Retaining its aura of mystery, it would henceforth always occupy an alluring place in the minds of those eager for military ambition – and Caesar had set a goal and a precedent for subsequent members of the Julian family. Moreover his experiences – he had a number of close shaves at the hands not only of the British but also of the elements – provided practical lessons for a future expeditionary commander.

Caesar had also set important precedents for intervention in Britain. He had received the surrender of powerful kings and accepted the friendship of others. A tribute – or annual tax – to be paid to Rome had been imposed. He had also installed as king of the Trinovantes of Essex a young prince who had fled to him in Gaul. The father of this prince had been killed by Cassivellaunus, the same Briton who was elected by the British confederation to lead them against Caesar – and who was now forbidden to interfere with the Trinovantes. Rome could, therefore, claim some sort of overlordship, the right to exact payments and an obligation to protect her friends, if she chose to move. (Rome rarely did so in fact, unless it was in her own interest: many small countries under her nominal protection failed to appreciate this basic fact of ancient life, with unfortunate consequences.) But precedent, we may remember, was important to the Romans, and after Caesar they had ample.

For two decades after Caesar, the attention of the Roman world was monopolized by the series of civil wars that brought the Republic to an end and put Caesar's adopted heir Octavian (later to assume the name Augustus) into power. Caesar had himself taken no action when his erstwhile Gallic friend Commius, whom he had installed as king of the Atrebates in Gaul, joined the great revolt. The crushing of that revolt saw Commius in flight to Britain – where he had earlier been used as Caesar's agent – to found a dynasty among the British Atrebates. The lack of Roman interest in Britain at this time is understandable. More interesting for us is that we are now beginning to identify tribes and plot the history of dynasties. Commius' own case is particularly intriguing. His rule over a Roman-devised 'client' kingdom of Gallic Atrebates and the Morini of the Channel coast north of the Seine had put him in control of much of the area through which the routes from the main concentration of 'Belgae', straddling the Meuse, ran towards Britain. Somewhat earlier than Caesar, there seems to have been the beginning of a movement from the Belgic part of Gaul into Britain which probably accelerated as Caesar's conquests progressed, establishing, at the least, related royal houses in Britain.

In the course of the first century BC, 'Belgic' culture became dominant in southern Britain, even among tribes themselves not Belgic. The pattern of life was changing. The division of labour in society became more pronounced, with more and more activities, such as pottery-making, becoming the preserve of craftsmen rather than domestic. British art reached a magnificent peak, especially in metalwork, all swirling motifs and fine enamelling, but it concentrated on the equipping of warrior chiefs and possibly the adornment of shrines. In the most Belgicized areas, hillforts tended to give way to large settlements on lower ground, sometimes with their approaches defended by great running earthworks. These have been seen as the forerunners of Roman towns, though some were more in the nature of royal residences than urban in the contemporary Mediterranean sense. But for the future of the British landscape the most interesting change is the widespread emergence, particularly in the period between Caesar and Claudius (54 BC–AD 43), of a more permanent pattern of rural land settlement, with regular boundaries that suggest regular tenure. There is a growing feeling among archaeologists that this period may mark the beginning of a framework of land-division that has persisted to the present day. Those who worked and owned the land have certainly changed many times. The skeleton of the landscape, in this credible hypothesis, has survived into modern times.

In the year before his first expedition Caesar had fought and destroyed at sea the fleet of the Veneti of Brittany, whose ships had controlled the carrying trade between Armorica and south-west Britain. About this time, archaeology shows a dramatic switch in emphasis to the routes between Belgic Gaul and the south and east of Britain. Henceforth, the sea passages from the Seine to the Southampton area, the short crossings from Boulogne to Kent, and the route from the Rhine and the Low Countries to the estuaries of Essex were paramount. It is not, perhaps, surprising to find that the greatest wealth and sophistication were now in these areas of Britain. From 12 BC, indeed, when Augustus launched his armies on the conquest of Holland and Germany, the new importance of the northern links with Britain must have further sharply increased. Although in the long run Augustus' attempt to extend the empire to the Elbe failed, from this time large Roman armies were permanently on the Rhine. Britain was exporting corn, hides, cattle, and iron to the empire, all items of vital importance to the Roman military effort. Recent research has indicated that the technologically efficient British agriculture was producing, at least in grain, a large surplus over the subsistence needs of its people. We may reasonably surmise that the increasing wealth, the changes in society, and even the new pattern of British agriculture were stimulated, perhaps even caused, by the opportunities offered by the needs of the army of the Rhine and the emerging civil markets of the new Roman provinces across the Channel.

In his early days Augustus was acutely conscious of the legacy of Caesar's memory and the urgent need to establish a military reputation for himself. Even before his final defeat of Mark Antony he seems to have planned an invasion of Britain; and at least two more attempts were made to put it into effect. All were frustrated by more pressing

2a. *The British aristocracy.* Roman silver cup decorated with vine leaves and olives, one of a group of silver vessels of Italian workmanship of the Augustan period, probably imported before the Claudian invasion, found at Hockwold, Norfolk

demands. After 26 BC, however, he was content to let the imminent conquest of Britain remain an uncorrected impression that served as useful propaganda at Rome, while developing diplomatic relations that may have sprung out of negotiations we know were already in progress, perhaps to re-establish Caesar's taxation. Strabo, an author writing late in Augustus' reign or under his successor Tiberius, confirms that the Britons were paying heavy customs dues to Rome on their import and export trade. He seems to reflect a party line that sought to justify the shift in policy away from invasion when he claims that Rome forbore to make the easy conquest of Britain because taxation without occupation was more profitable. The Britons, he adds significantly, posed no military threat.

2b. *The British aristocracy.* Chain intended for a chain-gang, possibly from the pre-Conquest slave-trade. Found among an Iron Age votive deposit, Llyn Cerrig, Anglesey, but thought to originate in East Anglia

Commius was succeeded on his British throne by a son, Tincommius, and around 15 BC there seems to have been a reversal of attitude which put this important kingdom at the British end of the Seine–Southampton route into friendship with Rome. The reason may have been the growing power of one British tribe, the Catuvellauni, centred in Hertfordshire. Whether they had recently coalesced from smaller clans or had already been the force behind Cassivellaunus is uncertain; but the history of Britain up to the Claudian conquest is now dominated by Catuvellaunian expansion. For the time being, however, Rome chose to turn a blind eye. Even the expulsion of Tincomarus and another British king, and their seeking refuge with Augustus, were only treated by Rome as support for the Augustan claim to exercise virtual sway over Britain, propaganda for internal consumption. Indeed, there is every sign the Catuvellauni were careful not to display open hostility. The balance was mutually profitable to the governing classes on both sides.

British aristocrats were enjoying the imports from the empire, while the list of exports that the Roman author thinks worthy of mention shows that the Britons were not only paying for these luxuries with supplies important to the army: by sending gold, silver, slaves, and hunting-dogs they had also become a source of commodities of direct interest to the emperor himself and to the rich at Rome. After disaster in Germany in AD 9, Augustus and his successor Tiberius erected non-intervention outside the empire into a principle – the absolute opposite of previous Augustan practice. It must, however, be a measure of the satisfactory nature of the working relationship that Cunobelinus, Shakespeare's Cymbeline, now king of the Catuvellauni, managed to avoid Roman retribution even when he took over the territory of Caesar's old protégés, the Trinovantes, and transferred the centre of his kingdom to Colchester. He now had command of the lucrative route to the Rhine. Within Britain he could cut the supply of their status symbols to other British princes at will; and whether by conquest or other means the power and influence of his kingdom continued to expand.

Chapter 2
The Roman Conquest

The state of mutual toleration, satisfactory as it doubtless was for Rome and the Catuvellauni – but perhaps not so welcome to other Britons – started to crumble when the unstable Gaius (Caligula) succeeded Tiberius. At some point in this period, Cunobelinus expelled one of his sons, who eventually fled to the emperor, to whom he made a formal act of submission. Gaius not only claimed the surrender of Britain; he also gave orders for an invasion. These he subsequently countermanded, but only at the last minute, and it is this that is important. The staff work had been done, the whole massive process of build-up to an invasion had been gone through, not as manoeuvres but as a real operation, and the Roman public had been reminded of unfinished business. Everything lay ready for a more determined hand.

The murder of Gaius hoisted unceremoniously to the throne his uncle Claudius, previously ignored by the rest of the imperial family under the mistaken notion that he was of defective intelligence. In fact, he combined common sense, an original mind bordering on the eccentric, a professional interest in history, and a profound veneration for Roman tradition. Faced soon after his elevation by a serious military revolt, the need to establish his reputation with the troops and gain respect at Rome must have been obvious to him. Such a man could hardly miss the chance of military glory offered by Britain and the opportunity not only to carry out the invasion cancelled by Augustus and Gaius before him

3a. *The army under the early Empire*. The legions: tombstone of Marcus Favonius Facilis, a centurion of the Twentieth, buried at Colchester. The stone was overturned during the Boudiccan revolt and consequently preserved intact

3b. *The army under the early Empire.* The auxiliary troops: bronze parade helmet with decorative face-mask, used in formal cavalry exercises. From Ribchester, Lancashire

but even to outdo Julius Caesar himself. Personal and family reputation could not be better served.

There was a pretext, too – and one which could be referred back to sound precedent and provided a strategic reason for intervention. Cunobelinus was now dead, and his realm had fallen into the hands of two aggressive sons – Caratacus and Togodumnus. The eastern entrance to Britain was, therefore, unreliable. In the south, pressure on Tincomarus' old kingdom had reduced it to a rump on the coast: now that entrance, too, closed when an internal coup expelled Tincomarus' successor, Verica. The latter, in the time-honoured fashion, also fled to the emperor. All Britain seemed to be turning hostile, and the valuable traffic between it and the empire was threatened. Like Caesar, Claudius could respond to an appeal from a British prince.

17

Caesar had relied upon inspired generalship and the devotion of the troops who had long served under him. The new standing regular army that Augustus and his successors had created still depended on generalship, but was more firmly based on meticulous organization and training and the permanence of its institutions. At this period, the legions, the backbone of the army, recruited only from Roman citizens, still drew most of their men from Italy. Gradually, the citizen colonies founded in the older provinces outside Italy were to provide men for the military career. Each legion had an establishment of something over 5,000 men, mostly heavy infantry, backed by small cavalry contingents, catapults, and other engines of war. The legions also provided a wide range of skilled craftsmen and administrators; and individual soldiers, all of whom were required to read and write, could be used on a vast range of government tasks. The 'auxiliary' units were, in the first half of the first century AD, evolving from native irregulars under their own chieftains into regular regiments of provincials, mostly non-citizen, but with Roman commanders. These regiments were normally 500 strong, cavalry, infantry, or mixed, with status and pay inferior to those of the legions. Both legionaries and auxiliaries, however, enjoyed those extreme rarities in the ancient world, a regular money wage, an assured career, and provision for retirement. Education, training, and opportunities for self-advancement – not to mention self-enrichment – made the army a major force in social mobility. Both serving and retired soldiers were persons of consequence in their communities. Auxiliaries automatically received Roman citizenship on retirement and their sons were eligible to join the legions. These units thus provided a continuous process of turning unlettered barbarians into literate Roman citizens and were a major element in the assimilation of new peoples into the empire.

The force assembled to sail to Britain in AD 43 comprised four legions and about the same number of auxiliary troops, around 40,000 men in all. Facing this disciplined machine, the British forces retained their old character. The permanent warriors were the aristocracy; their favourite weapon was the chariot, which they used for rapid transport in and out of battle and in the handling of which their drivers were extremely skilled. The exact status of the cavalry is uncertain: they were probably men who could provide their own horses, but it is not clear that their prime occupation in life was fighting. The mass of the British armies was the levies, summoned from the farms. Unlike the armoured Romans, Britons mostly wore little or no body protection and depended on speed, impetus, and the long slashing sword. Before they could get near to Romans in battle order they were liable to lose many men to the clouds of Roman javelins; and in hand-to-hand combat their long blades were at a disadvantage faced with the closed ranks and short stabbing swords of the enemy infantry. Successes by these Celtic troops against the Romans were usually gained in surprise attacks, in ambushes, and when overwhelming detached units by sheer numbers. They could rarely match the legions in pitched battle, and Roman commanders aimed to force them out into the open or to pen them behind ramparts where Roman siegecraft and artillery could beat them down or starve them out. But perhaps their greatest disadvantage in the face of the Romans was that as farmer-soldiers they could only stay in the field for a short part of the year. If they were not sent home, the population starved. The supply system of the Roman army, on the contrary, permitted it to campaign as long as the weather permitted, and to build fortified, well-stocked camps in which to sit out each winter. Such a system permitted a war to be carried on for year after year, and provided the basis for the garrisoning required for permanent occupation. Faced with such an opponent, it is remarkable that the British resisted so long and so hard.

The invasion met with fierce resistance from some of the British tribes. Others, no doubt not sorry to see the Catuvellaunian hegemony in southern Britain destroyed, surrendered easily or joined the Romans. The campaign was crowned by the submission of eleven British kings to the emperor and his triumphant entry into Colchester, for which he had joined his advancing forces, complete with elephants. His delight was marked by the revival of ancient rituals once performed by Republican victors and the proud proclamation of the extension of empire, in which the Conquest of Ocean once more figured large (and that was no hollow boast: the army had at first refused to sail).

The Romanization of Britain

By AD 47 the Claudian armies occupied Britain as far as the Severn and the Trent. The work of organizing Britain as a regular province was now in progress. Its governorship enjoyed high status. It was reserved for ex-consuls and carried with it the command of an exceptionally large group of legions. In its first century-and-a-half as a province, men of particular distinction were regularly chosen. It was not only a military challenge where reputations could be won, but – though we shall never have the figures to compare income from Britain with expenditure on its defence and administration – it was regarded as a land of natural abundance as late as the fourth century. By AD 47, indeed, the exploitation of Britain's mineral resources – one of the chief objectives of victory – had begun (the silver-bearing lead of the Mendips was being mined under state control by this date). It might have saved Rome much trouble and expense if she had limited her conquest to the area she already controlled; but it is very doubtful whether Roman ambition could long have been restrained, even if the warlike and unstable tribes of the north and Wales had not been a threat to the peaceful development of the south. As it was, the events of the next two or three years committed Rome to a different course.

Roman practice in the provinces was always to shift as much of the burden of administration on to loyal locals as soon as might be. The Claudian intention seems to have been to employ 'client' kings as far as possible – the most economical method, where they were reliable. A substantial part of the south, including Verica's old kingdom, was put in the hands of one Cogidubnus or Togidubnus, who may not have been a native Briton. The Iceni of Norfolk were kept as 'allies'; and an

4. Roman fort planted in the corner of a British hillfort, seen from the air at Hod Hill, Dorset, in the region where the future Emperor Vespasian overran 30 native strongholds in AD 43

5. Bronze head from a public statue of the Emperor Claudius, found in the River Alde, Suffolk, and probably looted from Colchester during the revolt of Boudicca

understanding was reached beyond the border of Roman rule with Cartimandua, queen of the Brigantes (a vast grouping of clans that encompassed most of northern England), with the object of securing the province from attack from the north. One success of this policy was when Cartimandua handed over the fugitive Caratacus to Claudius; another was the enduring loyalty of Cogidubnus, which was almost certainly of critical importance during later crises in Britain.

The rest of the province the governor would expect to administer chiefly through the tribes, reorganized as Roman local government units (*civitates*) with their nobles formed into councils and holding local magistracies – scaled-down versions of the Roman constitution, in fact, but often adapting existing institutions. In addition, throughout the province ran the writ of the chief financial secretary of Britain, the *procuratores provinciarum*. These provincial procurators reported direct to the emperor. This was natural enough, since they had particular responsibilities for crown land (the emperors automatically acquired the royal estates of defeated enemies, besides much else by inheritance or confiscation) and crown monopolies; but they also acted as a check on the governor, the emperor's military and judicial representative. Friction was not uncommon and not wholly unintentional.

The train of events that made it certain the province would not remain confined to the south started in AD 47 with the Roman response to raids from outside. Measures taken included not only counter-attacks but also the disarming of Britons within the province. This was bound to have come eventually, since civilians were forbidden to carry arms within the empire except in certain very limited circumstances – something that says much about everyday security in Roman times – but those who had voluntarily submitted to Rome had not expected it to apply to them. The Iceni revolted and were put down by force: the true status of the client kingdoms had now been made plain. The next step was the moving forward of the legion that had been stationed at Colchester and its replacement in AD 49 by a colony of Roman legionary veterans. This was intended as the seat of the Imperial Cult – the formal worship of Rome and the Imperial Family which focused the loyalty of the province – and the veterans were to act as a bulwark against possible revolt. In practice, Colchester was now an ungarrisoned civil city. Perhaps at the same moment, London was founded as a supply port. It is possible that from its beginning it was intended in due course to become the administrative centre of Britain as well. It was in all probability created as a deliberate act, rather than emerging out of a casual settlement of traders, as was formerly thought. The pre-eminence of the Essex coast was now challenged by the Thames, and London's position at the hub of the radiating system of main roads now being built, designed for official purposes, very soon made it also the business centre of the province.

The Boudiccan Revolt

The 50s were a decade of urban development. Only the agricultural hinterland remained largely unchanged, at least on the surface, and progress towards the universal adoption of the money economy was slow. By AD 60, however, with the governor, Suetonius Paullinus, about to subdue the troublesome tribes of North Wales, the province looked set to progress steadily. What went wrong? Why did the provincials, led by Rome's old friends the Iceni and Trinovantes, turn into a raging horde, set on destroying every trace of Rome?

We have only the Roman account, but it is enough to reveal maladministration ranging from the callously negligent to the undeniably criminal. Tacitus makes a general comment on the British character: 'The Britons bear conscription, the tribute, and their other obligations to the empire without complaint, provided there is no injustice. That they take extremely ill; for they can bear to be ruled by others but not to be their slaves.' The responsibility for the catastrophe cannot be confined to the procurator alone, the traditional villain of the piece. The governor has to take a share, and it cannot stop there. The young Nero, now on the throne, can hardly be blamed directly, for he was under the influence of his 'good' advisers, Burrus, the praetorian prefect, and the philosopher and dramatist Seneca. Of these two, it seems very likely that Seneca, at least, knew what was going on in Britain because he suddenly recalled, in a ruthless manner, large sums of money he had been lending to leading Britons at a high rate of interest. Reports coming out of Britain may well have indicated unrest that might put his investment at risk. In the event, the action fuelled the flames. There are two main threads to the grievances, represented respectively by the Iceni and the Trinovantes. At his death, Boudicca's husband, Prasutagus, the client king of the Iceni, had left half his possessions to the emperor, expecting that this would protect his kingdom and family. Agents of the procurator and of the governor, however, had treated this as if it were the unconditional surrender of an enemy. The king's property was confiscated, nobles were expelled from their estates, and taxation and conscription enforced. The Trinovantes were suffering other insults. The main burden of the Imperial Cult, designed to promote loyalty to the emperor, had fallen on their nobles, while the Roman colonists – significantly with the encouragement of serving soldiers – seized their lands and treated them with contempt. They (and probably the aristocracies of other *civitates*) were facing financial ruin, the last straw being the reclaiming of grants made by Claudius and the recall of Seneca's loans. The Imperial Cult, as represented by the Temple of the Deified Claudius at Colchester, was, ironically, the focus of British hatred.

In answer to Boudicca's protests, she was flogged and her daughters raped. Rousing her own tribe and her Trinovantian neighbours and carrying other *civitates* with her (but clearly not Cogidubnus), she swept through southern Britain, burning Colchester, London, and Verulamium (near St Albans), torturing every Roman or Roman sympathizer she could catch, and inflicting devastating defeats on the few Roman units that had been left in that part of the country. The governor only just avoided the total loss of the province. After the eventual victory when he had brought her to battle, his retribution was all the more extreme. For a while it looked as if the ruin of the province of Britain would now ironically be achieved at Roman hands. Nero, indeed, at one stage in his reign – possibly earlier, perhaps now – had been inclined to abandon Britain altogether. In the end two factors saved the province: the intervention of a remarkable new provincial procurator, Classicianus, himself of Gallic origin, and the recall to Rome of the governor.

The recovery that occupied Britain for the decade after Boudicca was genuine but unspectacular. There is some evidence that under the last governor appointed by Nero it was beginning to accelerate. But the outbreak of civil war across the empire in AD 69 ('The Year of the Four Emperors') revived the spectre of generals fighting for supremacy. However, the outcome of the wars brought in a vigorous new administration in the persons of the Flavian emperors. For Britain, this spelled provincial renewal and the expansion of Roman power. As Tacitus says, 'Now come great generals and magnificent armies, and with them the hopes of our enemies fall into ruin.'

While the Roman world had been distracted by the civil wars, a fresh outbreak of strife among the Brigantes had lost Cartimandua her kingdom and embroiled the Roman army. The north of Britain was no longer secure. The old policy of client kingship, already shaken by Boudicca and previous Brigantian disturbances, was finally discredited. Within a few years even Cogidubnus was probably pensioned off to live in the splendid villa of Fishbourne. By AD 83 or 84 a succession of first-rate governors had carried Roman arms to the far north of Scotland and garrisons to the edge of the Highlands – and were pressing ahead with Romanization. Tacitus, in describing the work of his father-in-law Agricola, uses words that characterize the Flavian period as a whole:

In order to encourage a truculent population that dwelled in scattered settlements (and was thus only too ready to fall to fighting) to live in a peaceful and inactive manner by offering it the pleasures that would follow on such a way of living, Agricola urged these people privately, and helped them officially, to build temples, public squares with public buildings (*fora*), and private houses (*domus*). He praised those who responded quickly, and severely criticized laggards. In this way, competition for public recognition took the place of compulsion. Moreover he had the children of the leading Britons educated in the civilized arts and openly placed the natural ability of the Britons above that of the Gauls, however well trained. The result was that those who had once shunned the Latin language now sought fluency and eloquence in it. Roman dress, too, became popular and the toga was frequently seen. Little by little there was a slide toward the allurements of degeneracy: assembly-rooms (*porticus*), bathing establishments and smart dinner parties. In their inexperience the Britons called it civilization when it was really all part of their servitude.

To a certain extent this urbanization under the Flavians was less than completely successful. The core of its more securely based development can reasonably be associated with the visit of the Emperor Hadrian to Britain in person in 122, when existing schemes were revived or replaced and vast new works put in hand. But, looked at in longer perspective, the period from AD 70 to the 160s is the age when Britain truly became Roman and its lasting features as part of the empire emerged. Central to this absorption into the Roman system was the more or less universal devolution of the burden of routine administration to the local aristocracies that replaced the client kingdoms. It was crucially important to this policy to win over the native aristocracy whose confidence had been so disastrously lost in the reign of Nero, and it is in this context that Tacitus must be read.

Town and City

Archaeologically, we can observe in the late first century and the beginning and middle of the second century the development of the cities and towns of Roman Britain to their full extent. The administrative centres of the *civitates* were provided with civic centres: the forum and public hall (*basilica*) that provided market, law courts, civic offices, and council chambers; the public baths which in the Roman world provided the urban centre for relaxation and social life; engineered water supplies; public monuments honouring imperial figures and local worthies; and, in a number of cases, theatres or amphitheatres. This archaeological evidence is all the more significant in that in the empire it was normally the local notables themselves (in council or as individuals) who paid for such amenities, not the State or emperor. Occasionally, a great private patron with local connections might favour the town with a benefaction or by acting as friend at court. Only in fairly rare and well-publicized instances did emperors take a part, directly or through their representatives.

The urban expansion could not, of course, have rested solely on the basis of a relatively small native aristocracy taught to accept Roman ways. Indeed, the fact that this spread of town life was followed by the appearance of many 'villas' in the countryside – at this stage mainly modest but comfortable Roman houses, often replacing native homesteads – indicates that the British gentry retained their connections with the land. Most probably they were still chiefly resident on their estates, and many ordinary farmers shared their prosperity. In this period, too, veterans discharged from the legions were principally concentrated in the small number of cities deliberately founded to take them: Colchester, Lincoln, and Gloucester. The flourishing of the towns as a whole, therefore, depended equally on the emergence, well attested, of a lively urban population made up of officials, the professions, traders, and skilled artisans.

Some of these people, particularly among the craftsmen and traders, were immigrants or visitors from other parts of the empire, and many officials were on short-term postings to the province. Nevertheless, the population of Roman Britain remained overwhelmingly indigenous. The ranks of the Roman army, too, were increasingly recruited from the provinces in which units were stationed: gradually Britons who had been, like the mass of their fellows, without the distinctive Roman citizenship when they joined the army, must, as discharged veterans with their grants of citizenship and substantial gratuities, have formed an important part of the solid centre of the Romanized society now emerging. In the towns, slaves were set up in business by their masters; and the frequent use in the Roman world of the power to set slaves free or allow them to purchase their liberty expanded the skilled labour force and added to the body of businessmen. Whatever the condition of the agricultural labourer, social mobility was high in the skilled and educated portion of society. Whilst the vast bulk of the ordinary people of Britain undoubtedly remained on the land – and we have to recall that industry, too, was largely concentrated in the countryside – the towns of the Early Empire came to provide centres of public life,

Map 1. Second-century Britain

exchange and services for the rural hinterland, and wide opportunities of advancement at different levels of society.

Hadrian's revival of flagging Flavian initiatives was thus of major importance. But his impact on the province was great in other ways. A man of restless and extraordinary character and energy, much of his reign was taken up with tours of the provinces. One of the few emperors deliberately to set himself against the tradition of expansion of the empire, he was personally unpopular with the Roman aristocracy and many of his vast enterprises were only partially successful, though whether due to internal opposition or to flaws in planning is not always clear. In Britain there are at least three major examples. Hadrian's Wall was constructed on the line to which Roman forces had been withdrawn in stages over the 30 years since the extreme point of expansion, partly because of demands for troops elsewhere, partly due to fairly serious local reverses in the field. Such a policy suited Hadrian's general inclination to limit the empire, and the design of the Wall was brilliantly original. In part because of this, however, detailed study of its early history has revealed a remarkable series of changes of plan within Hadrian's reign; and it must have cost many times the original estimates of the expenditure and time required for completion. Similarly, the agricultural colonization of the Fenlands of East Anglia involved water engineering on a grand scale, yet many of the farms failed after only a few years. Hadrianic London, too, saw the demolition of the substantial Flavian forum and basilica and their replacement with a complex twice the normal size. In Gaul and elsewhere Hadrian intervened to help cities erect public buildings. In London this was probably related to the presence of the emperor himself during his visit to Britain in AD 122, which is supported by the erection of a permanent fort in the city at about this time – something almost unparalleled in the cities of the empire outside Rome. But when a great fire had swept through London later in Hadrian's reign, the effort to reconstruct areas that had been devastated was relatively short-lived, and in the later years of the second century London shows signs of urban decay.

6a. Hadrian's Wall and Housesteads Fort: the Wall joins the front of the fort at the right-hand corners. In the centre is the headquarters building, with the commanding officer's house on the left and a pair of granaries on the right. Behind lies the military hospital. In the bottom right corner are three barracks and, bottom left, a latrine block. Outside the fort can be seen a few of the many houses, shops, and temples of the dependent civil settlement

6b. The Antonine Wall in Scotland: Second-century cavalry trooper riding down barbarian enemies, depicted on a 'distance slab' recording a sector constructed by a named unit, the Second Legion *Augusta*. From Bridgeness, on the Firth of Forth

Hadrian's frontier line from the Tyne to Solway Firth represents broadly the limit within which the province settled for most of its history. Yet there were at least three major wars of conquest northwards subsequent to Hadrian, two of them commanded in person by emperors; and for long periods garrisons were maintained at points beyond the Hadrianic line and a degree of control exercised. Indeed, within months of his death in AD 138 plans were in hand to launch a new invasion of Scotland; and by 142 the armies of his generally unmilitary successor, Antoninus Pius, had, like those of Claudius, provided him with a conquest in the prestigious field of Britain. Scotland as far as the Firth of Tay was in Roman hands, and work commenced on a new, shorter, and more simply built linear barrier to run from the Forth to the

Clyde. Elaborate commemorative stone relief sculptures, set at positions along what we know as the Antonine Wall, record the confident mood of what was to be the last period of unconstrained expansion of Roman rule.

In this Early Antonine period, the developments we have seen in town and country reached their first peak. Elsewhere, the empire is generally considered to have been enjoying a golden age of tranquillity and prosperity. In Britain the economic system of the Early Empire had been fully accepted, based on a money economy and large-scale, long-distance trade. Culturally, Roman fashions were dominant, and classical art and decoration widely adopted. Perhaps, historically, the most important artistic impact on the Britons of Roman conquest was the introduction of figurative styles, particularly in sculpture, wall-painting, and mosaic, but also in a vast range of minor arts and crafts – jewellery, pottery, furniture, and household goods of every description. First-rate works of art from Roman Britain are relatively few compared with, say, southern Gaul, but they do exist. The middle range of material is, however, quite plentiful and it is abundantly clear that mass-produced articles were freely available. It is these, rather than the few works of high art that have survived, that reveal an everyday revolution in the way of life since the Pre-Roman Iron Age. Roman pottery alone reveals the existence of a 'throwaway society' that is quite different from what went before or came after.

Religion

Because it affected the deepest levels of consciousness, religion provides the most telling evidence for the assimilation of Roman and native. Roman Britain was a religious kaleidoscope, ranging from the formal rites of the Roman State – Jupiter, Juno, and Minerva, in particular – and the Imperial Cult that had more recently been grafted on to it, through wide range of religions imported both from the neighbouring West and from the East, to the local Celtic cults. People from overseas often retained their own favourite practices: Diodora, a Greek priestess, dedicated an altar at Corbridge in her own language to the demi-god Heracles of Tyre; soldiers from the Netherlands set up others at Housesteads on Hadrian's Wall to their native goddesses the Alaisiagae, Baudihillia and Friagabis, Beda and Fimmilena. But for our purpose the most significant are the 'conflations' or amalgamations of classical and Celtic deities. This was a difficult and uncertain process, since Celtic religion identified its deities much less clearly than Roman, but it was very widespread. That its acceptance was more than superficial is clear, for example, from an altar in the great complex of temple and baths at Bath erected to Sulis Minerva – the native healing spirit of the hot springs conflated with the Roman goddess of wisdom – by Lucius Marcius Memor, *haruspex*. The function of the *haruspices* was divination of the future from the entrails of sacrificial animals. This ancient practice, held in the highest honour, went back to very early Etruscan strands in Italian religion, yet it is here related to a half-Celtic deity. Again, on Hayling Island, a major shrine of the Pre-Roman Iron Age – more than likely associated with the kingship of Verica – was rebuilt subsequently in Roman materials, perhaps by an architect from Roman Gaul commissioned by Cogidubnus. It is a particularly fine example of a very large class of distinctive shrines known to archaeologists as 'Romano-Celtic temples', found right across Britain, Gaul, and Roman Germany, and quite clearly the expression in Roman architectural terms of a pre-existing type peculiar to the Celtic peoples. They are instantly recognizable, being square, circular, or polygonal structures, usually box-like with a concentric 'ambulatory', and often set within enclosed precincts which may sometimes have preserved sacred groves from pre-Roman times.

At a much less formal level we find in Weardale a cavalry officer giving thanks to Silvanus (a Celtic rural god in Roman guise) for 'a remarkably fine boar no one had previously been able to catch', or at Greta Bridge two ladies setting up an altar to the local nymph. These are typical of the deep belief of both Celts and Romans that every place had its own deity. Romans found no difficulty in accepting these deities of place in the lands they conquered. Indeed, they showed real anxiety to find out their names and honour them, as a precaution if nothing else. The darker side was a belief in ghosts and the need to placate them. Here we are at the heart of Roman religion, very congenial to the Britons, the animistic belief in the localized spirits of hearth, home, family, and ancestors, and of places and objects outside, which long pre-dated the public adoption of the classical gods of Olympus. The black element is represented archaeologically by written curses, some still sickening to read. From Clothall near Baldock comes a lead plate bearing a message written backwards (a practice common in magic), declaring that 'Tacita is hereby cursed, and this curse shall reveal her to be putrefying like rotting blood'. It is surely not just chance that excavation of a temple at Uley in Gloucestershire has approximately doubled the total of curse-bearing tablets known from the entire Roman world. The Britons, we are told by a classical source, were obsessed with ritual. The specifically Roman contributions were to provide new artistic and architectural forms to express religious feelings, and written language in which to make those sentiments clear and permanent. Roman religious practice, with that same sense that informed Roman law, depended on the exact performance of every act and word. The care with which the Romano-Briton phrased his dedications and curses demonstrates how well the new capacity to set wording down indelibly accorded with his own ritual inclinations.

After the invasion of Scotland, Antoninus Pius waged no more aggressive wars anywhere in the Roman world, and in the 160s the mood began to change. In Britain something had gone seriously wrong around 158. There is some evidence that the Brigantes had to be suppressed, a situation perhaps made possible by premature thinning out of troops on the ground in the Pennines under the demands of the occupation of southern Scotland; and it seems the Antonine Wall itself was temporarily lost. A brief reoccupation of Scotland, perhaps after a punitive campaign (though the chronology of this period in the north is exceptionally obscure) was followed by a definitive return to the Hadrianic line. In the reign of the next emperor, Marcus Aurelius, barbarian pressure on the frontiers of the empire generally became serious. The initiative, though Rome did not recognize it for centuries, had passed from her.

Defence and Security

For a traveller arriving from the Continent, there was one particularly striking fashion in which Britain would have seemed different from northern Gaul, whose development it had in so many ways paralleled, allowing for the century less of time it had been under Roman rule. The permanent military presence would have made him aware that a primary concern of governors in Britain was always one of defence: there were three legions, two in the west in fortresses at Chester and at Caerleon in South Wales, and one in the north at York, together with a very large number of auxiliary units, many occupied in containing the nominally pacified tribesmen of the hills inside the province by means of a network of forts and patrolled roads. But the most visible difference in the south was the presence of town walls. The building of these walls was not (other than at one period) a general response to a particular crisis. It was a leisurely process, starting in the first century with towns such as Winchester and Verulamium and still in progress in the 270s. By the early second century the three prestigious colonies had walls; and an element of civic rivalry may have stirred elsewhere. The main reason for their walls, however, had to be something sufficiently important to overcome the reluctance of Roman emperors to allow the construction of fortifications that might be held by an enemy or insurgents (locals paid for the walls, but the emperor's express permission was required) and permanent enough for the process to continue even though Britain was several times implicated in major challenges to authority. Lack of defences to the villas rules out a disorderly countryside or fear of peasant revolt. The reason must be the same factor that kept the legions in the province and the auxiliary units stationed where they were: apprehension of barbarian incursion from outside and risings in the hills within the province. The cities and towns, lying on the main roads, were the obvious targets for tribes or war parties on the move. In the ancient world, city walls were more or less impregnable except to armies with sophisticated siege machinery and the logistic support necessary to sustain a prolonged siege, or where the attackers had friends within the town. Against tribesmen, therefore, walls were a first-rate form of civic defence; and their prevalence in Britain must indicate a much greater awareness of threat than was abroad in Gaul.

The walls, however, took a long time to build, and a speedier remedy was sometimes needed. An indication of impending crisis is the appearance on a large number of urban sites in Britain of earthwork defences, apparently in the second half of the second century. At Cirencester, for example, an earth rampart was thrown up to link monumental stone city gates and interval towers already built, as if an urgent decision had been taken to interrupt the leisurely construction programme and put the defences into immediate commission. Of the various candidates that have been proposed for this period of crisis, the most likely seems the outbreak in the north around 180 which included barbarian penetration of the frontier, reported widespread damage, and the death of a Roman general. A much less likely context is the candidacy of a governor of Britain, Clodius Albinus, for the imperial throne in the years 193–7.

The events surrounding his attempt, however, herald a new age in the history of the empire, in the course of which Britain's fortunes diverged much more sharply from those of neighbouring Gaul. Marcus Aurelius' great wars on the Danube, which in the event marked the beginning of the unrelenting barbarian pressure in the West, might, had not his death intervened, have led to his achieving his aim of conquering Central Europe north of the Danube. Instead, the year 180 saw the breakdown of the system of nominating successors to the imperial throne that had produced a century of moderate and extremely able emperors. The accession of Marcus' dreadful son, Commodus, coincided in Britain with the outbreak of the serious warfare in the north mentioned above. In Britain and elsewhere, attempts to tighten up discipline in the Roman army had ironic consequences. A short period that saw a return to a rapid succession of murdered emperors and fresh outbreaks of civil war ended not only with the army in a much stronger position in society but with other profound changes in the system. The final victor, after the defeat of Clodius Albinus in Gaul, was the immensely tough Septimius Severus. But, far from bringing the army back to the disciplined loyalty of the previous hundred years, Severus' strategy for the survival of his own dynasty was to subordinate everything to the interests of the troops.

The third-century emperors abandoned the pretence of rule by consent. The senatorial class, which the second-century emperors had, with varying degrees of sincerity, tried to keep involved in the responsibilities of government, both civil and military, lost ground to the career soldiers who were providing the professional officers whom the army increasingly required. The old distinction between Roman citizens and provincials without the citizenship, already fading as more and more of the latter won Roman status, was now swept away and replaced by a new class structure before the law – an upper division (*honestiores*) and a lower (*humiliores*). Significantly, soldiers fell into the former category. By the middle of the century, rampant inflation had severely damaged confidence in the currency; and the old economic pattern of major centres of production serving very large areas of the Roman world by means of long-distance trade based on a money economy was tending to be replaced by more localized industries.

For the first quarter of the third century, Septimius Severus and his dynasty seemed to offer a renewed stability, even if one based on military autocracy. But that in itself was an insecure foundation. In the middle of the century, one assassinated emperor followed another in rapid succession as army officers changed their allegiances. The old, fatal weaknesses of personal ambition and the readiness of the Roman soldier to follow his commander were unchecked. At this point almost total disaster struck as barbarians attacked in both East and West. In the East a newly invigorated Persian Empire captured the Emperor Valerian, while successive Germanic invasions wrecked the unwalled cities of Gaul and prevented Rome from any further shielding of towns and territories across the Rhine with a permanent military presence. By 260 much of the empire was in a sorry state.

It was formerly believed that Britain had been similarly devastated when Clodius Albinus' unsuccessful campaign on the Continent against Severus was supposed to have stripped Britain of troops and opened the way for a major barbarian invasion. The archaeology will no longer support such a hypothesis. Problems with the tribes beyond the northern frontier towards the end of Severus' life did, however, give him a reason to choose Britain on which to launch a new war of conquest. There was no slackening of Roman ambition. Here the intention was the total subjugation of Scotland, to complete the conquest of the island. There is, indeed, cause to think that the interest of the Severan House in Britain revived a province that had become somewhat run down. Perhaps in connection with the imperial visit itself, London was tidied up, given new public buildings, provided with the longest circuit of walls in Britain and, at some time in the Severan period, its waterfront magnificently re-equipped with continuous quays running for more than half a mile. While the war was being planned, the imperial household itself probably settled at York. Much work had already been undertaken on the forts of the north behind the Wall, many of which seem to have been neglected, since the defeat of the barbarian intruders in the early 180s. There is some reason to think that York itself had assumed some of the governmental functions formerly located at London, perhaps when the Antonine reoccupation of Scotland extended the lines of communication. Sometime early in the third century the city that had grown up alongside the legionary fortress was dignified with the honorary rank of Roman colony. It is not, therefore, surprising to find London and York being chosen as twin capitals when, at some not entirely certain point in the Severan period, Britain was divided into two provinces. This was in line with a new policy to reduce the number of legions under the command of any one provincial governor and thus the temptation to revolt.

The planned conquest of Scotland was called off – but only after substantial successes – owing to the death of the emperor and the pressures on his successor. Security of the frontier was, however, accomplished. Britain as a whole shows every sign of having escaped the disasters of the age elsewhere. There was a slowing of new development, but the towns remained active and the villas were, if not expanded, kept up. Industry, if pottery is an indication, benefited from the problems of its rivals on the Continent. Some public work that might have been expected was not undertaken: restoration in the Fenlands after severe flooding, for example. But the defences of Britain continued to be refurbished, and new forts built on the south and east coast, at Brancaster and Reculver, probably for purposes of political control of the routes to the Continent and not yet indicative of an acute threat from sea-borne barbarians. In Gaul, AD 260 saw yet more trouble from the Germans – not yet by any means the worst – and the central government in Rome lost control. Germany, Gaul, Spain, and Britain adhered to an independent emperor, comprising together the 'Empire of the Gallic Provinces' (*Imperium Galliarum*). This grouping had been foreshadowed under Clodius Albinus and re-emerged later as a structural part of the restored empire. For the time being, however, possession of peaceful, prosperous Britain with its powerful and undamaged forces and its almost legendary propaganda value must have been a considerable comfort to the Gallic emperors.

Chapter 3
Britain under the Late Empire

In the 270s the imminent collapse of the empire – imminent, that is, with hindsight – was averted. Romans did not behave then or later as if Rome could ever fall. Emperors and would-be emperors or emperor-makers did not cease murdering one another, but a series of great soldier-emperors nevertheless restored the military balance against the barbarians, put down rival administrations, and began to repair the physical and institutional fabric of the State. This was done to such an effect that the imperial system was enabled to survive another two centuries in the West (and might have lasted much longer) and twelve in the East. In 274 Britain was brought back under the central government when the Emperor Aurelian eliminated the Gallic Empire. Britain's immediate fate, however, was very different from that of the Gallic part of the former independent north-western state. In 276 the towns of Gaul were still unwalled when, as a literary source tells us, the worst of the barbarian invasions yet saw the capture of fifty or sixty towns and their retaking by the Romans. In north-eastern France archaeology has revealed the abandonment in the late third century of villa after villa in what had been a region outstanding for its extraordinarily dense pattern of really large country houses and their estates. These houses were not to be reoccupied.

In Britain the contrast is acute. In the period 250–70 there are signs of a modest amount of building and none of universal neglect, while archaeologists are tending to date an increasing amount of new construction, particularly of villas or of enlargements and improvements to villas, to around 270–5 – for example in the villas of Witcombe and Frocester Court, on the western edge of the Cotswolds. An interesting hypothesis has been advanced that there was a 'flight of capital' from Gaul to Britain. As yet there is no positive evidence for this theory, but if modified a little it is attractive. It is certainly true that the great age of the Romano-British villa, long recognized as being at its peak in the fourth century, must have had its beginnings in the 270s. It seems unlikely, however, that landowners could have extracted their 'capital' from their ruined Gallic estates (in other words, sold them at a good price). When these estates were reoccupied at the end of the century it was as abandoned land given over to settlers imported by government. Behind the argument, however, lies too parochial a view of land ownership, an unspoken assumption that the typical provincial landowner possessed a single estate and lived in its villa most of the time. Possession of more than one estate was common among the upper classes of the Roman world, where wealth and status were quintessentially marked by landed property, sometimes in many parts of the empire simultaneously. For the pattern of Britain and Gaul at this period, it is thus much more likely that owners with land on both sides of the Channel decided to transfer their personal residences from their Gallic villas to their properties in what must have seemed an exceptionally secure haven in an age of extreme danger; and the movement may already have started among the more cautious under the Gallic Empire. Perhaps a small piece of circumstantial evidence is that when the cities of Gaul were finally walled after 276, the circuits, though very strong, were in general short (quite unlike Britain), sometimes more like those of very powerful fortresses than walled towns. This is just what one would expect if there were no longer enough magnates with active local interests who could be tapped for the funds to defend the whole urban area.

Architecturally, these Gallic fortress cities do have close relations in

Britain which are more or less contemporary, but these are not the towns. A number of new coastal fortresses were built in southern Britain with the same pattern of very high stone walls and massive projecting towers. At a much later date – in the fifth century – they are listed under a commander 'of the Saxon Shore', which has persistently suggested that they originated as a planned system of defence against Saxon sea-pirates. This is probably an anachronism. There is some reason to think that Aurelian's successor, Probus, created a tighter control of both sides of the Channel by establishing in Britain and Gaul similar strings of coastal forts; but the prime purpose has not been proven. The fact that Probus had more than once to quell serious moves against his authority in Britain may suggest that the 'Saxon Shore' had more at this stage to do with political security within the empire than frontier defence. Britain was an important asset – even more so in these straitened times – but control of the Channel was essential to its retention.

This fact was demonstrated in a remarkable fashion. In 287 a senior Roman officer named Carausius, who had been put in charge of a campaign to clear an infestation of pirates out of the Channel, came under strong suspicion of allowing the raids to happen and misappropriating the loot when it was subsequently seized by his fleet. Anticipating execution, Carausius rebelled and took control of Britain. Once again Britain was under the rule of a local emperor. This episode has attracted much romanticizing, but the fact is that neither Carausius nor other Romans before or after him who claimed the imperial title regarded Britain as something separate. Carausius is typical in blandly claiming on his coinage equality and fraternity with imperial colleagues, who, in fact, held the rest of the empire but with whom his fiction implied shared rule of the whole. The Carausian regime proved remarkably hard to dislodge, protected as it was by the sea. Carausius himself was unseated and murdered by Allectus, one of his own men, when he had lost a foothold on the Continent with the end of the siege of Boulogne in 293; but it was another three years before the central

43

Roman government could launch a successful invasion. The Channel had proved formidable again.

Reform under Diocletian

Despite the fact that an element of inspired seamanship and a good deal of luck contributed greatly to the defeat of Allectus – not to mention what looks very much like lack of enthusiasm for his cause on the part of the regular garrison of Britain – by 296 the rebel administration in Britain had faced a much more formidable central power. Major changes had taken place in the Roman State in those few years which move us into the period known as the 'Late Roman Empire'. The driving force was the Emperor Diocletian. Rooting himself in Roman precedent like Augustus, he initiated through his reforms a period of change that transformed the Roman State over half a century. He attempted to deal with the chronic political instability by creating a system of two senior emperors (*Augusti*) and two juniors as 'Caesars', with automatic succession. The individual provinces were once again reduced in size, and now grouped in 'dioceses', under a new tier of civilian officers known as *vicarii* to whom the governors (no longer commanding armies) were now made responsible. The frontiers were strengthened by approximately doubling the units of the army, under new commanders. Against domestic conspiracy or military revolt a deliberate attempt was made to create a greater aura around the persons of the emperors. The overall increases in the civil service were noted as phenomenal. The effects on art, fashion, and manners were hardly less pronounced.

The economic ravages of the century had been acute. Manpower shortages were now tackled by imposing rigid controls on the movement of labour, making many occupations hereditary. The problem was exceptionally severe on the land. There, the estate system which under the Late Republic had relied on a ready supply of cheap slaves from foreign wars had, in the course of the Early Empire, moved extensively to letting-out to large numbers of free tenant farmers on short leases. The disastrous economic conditions of the third century over large parts of the empire encouraged drift from the land. In reply, Diocletian virtually created a tied peasantry (the *coloni*) by law. Inflation was – ineffectually – tackled by detailed price legislation (on British duffel coats, rugs, and beer, for example). Persons in the public service were increasingly protected by being paid partially or wholly in kind. Troops, who had formerly had to buy their personal equipment out of their pay, were henceforth supplied from state factories, while officials' allowances came to be valued as much as their salaries. Taxation soared to meet the cost of reform; and the new rigidity of society had to be further tightened against attempted avoidance of the specific tax liabilities imposed on certain classes in the social hierarchy.

The new order must have arrived in full force in Britain soon after the reconquest in 296 by the Caesar in the West, Constantius I, the father of Constantine the Great. His timely rescue of London from a retreating force of Frankish mercenaries who had been in the pay of Allectus was a huge propaganda victory. It will be seen to be prophetic in more ways than one.

Most of the disorder seems to have been in the south, confined to the short campaign when Allectus was defeated. In the north, archaeological evidence for vigorous rebuilding of military installations initiated by Constantius seems to indicate more an intention for the future than repair of damage caused by enemies. The evidence suggests that a lengthy period of peace had allowed maintenance and manning to have low priority. Constantius had different ideas. Indeed, an unconvincing contemporary denial strengthens the impression that he had every intention, when opportunity offered, of launching another of those prestigious campaigns in Scotland that seem to have appealed so much to ambitious Roman emperors. Certainly, he lost no time after he became Augustus in preparing for such a war, and in 306 he was in the field. The sources claim a victory over the Picts (the first time the enemy in Scotland appears under this name); and pottery of the period found at Cramond at the eastern end of the Antonine Wall and from the old Severan fortress on the Tay suggests another sweep up the eastern side of the Highlands as his plan. Like Severus, Constantius returned to York and there died. Like Severus, he had had his successor with him.

Constantine the Great

In the elevation of Constantine the Great by the army, York can fairly be said to have witnessed one of the turning-points in history. It was a curiously haphazard affair, strongly influenced by a German king called Crocus who had accompanied Constantius as one of his officers – and was completely contrary to the spirit of Diocletian's settlement. It set off a chain of events that ended with Constantine as sole emperor, putting into supreme power a man quite unlike Diocletian in adhering little to the traditional past but like him in being capable of thinking and acting on the grandest scale. Constantine's innovations on the basis of Diocletian's conservative but immense reforms set patterns for centuries to come.

It has long been recognized that the first half of the fourth century was something of a 'golden age' for Roman Britain. We can now see that this was based on sound foundations from the previous century and continued trends already emerging in the 270s. This period of great prosperity certainly continued till the 340s, possibly until just after the middle of the century. It can legitimately be suspected that the most brilliant phase owed something to the favour of Constantine. There is some reason to suppose that, like his father, he returned to Britain and celebrated military success here. We certainly know that for part of his reign he promoted to major status the mint at London that had been set up by Carausius. It is not impossible, too, that it was he who was responsible for changing London's name to 'Augusta'; and some think that the superb river face of the walls of the fortress of York was a deliberate expression of the power of the man who had been proclaimed there, and who shared Hadrian's pleasure in vast architectural gestures.

The spirit of the age is typified by the great villas of fourth-century Britain. Socially and economically, the Late Empire in the West was marked by a polarization of wealth and to some extent power between the greater landed aristocracy on the one hand and emperor, court, and army on the other. These forces were often in conflict, but gradually tended to merge. Between them they left relatively little for the old urban middle class and the lesser gentry. Generally in the empire it was on the members of the local councils, the *curiales*, that the burden of paying for the new order fell most heavily. What had once been an honour now became a hereditary burden, and ways out were gradually sealed off by legislation.

Who, then, can have been the obviously wealthy inhabitants of the larger Romano-British villas? Some may have been rich citizens who had transferred themselves from elsewhere. If senators, or imperial officials of appropriate standing, they would have been exempt from the duties of *curiales*. Yet the curious persistence in Britain of forms of Latin indicative of educated speech but tending to be peculiar to the island does suggest that the native aristocracy remained a significant element in society. It is highly probable that they had, exceptionally, not been too badly hit in the previous century. It is tempting to wonder, too, whether Constantine may not have shown them special favour.

Like the eighteenth-century English country house, to which they may in many respects reasonably be compared, these villas vary in plan, complexity, and size. Certain features are generally present, notably construction in permanent materials, central heating (in the form of wood-, sometimes coal-fired hot air systems), glazing, tessellated floors, and very often one or more complete bath suites. Agricultural buildings normally adjoin, and like their Georgian counterparts it is probable that most had land attached. It is clear from Roman literature that the degree and importance to the individual occupier of any particular villa of its 'economic' activity could vary enormously, from being a major source of income to little more than an amusement. Significantly, the great houses such as Woodchester, Chedworth, or North Leigh did not stand alone, but formed the top of a very broad pyramid of villas. The modest villas that had developed in earlier times out of Iron Age farms survived, improved, or were replaced by new middle-range and small villas. This is the best evidence for the survival of a solid gentry in Britain. Some villas, it is true, disappear; but this is in the natural order of things even in a completely settled age. It is more important that in this age the villa is becoming a more prominent feature of the landscape, not less.

It has been observed that villas often display duplication in their main facilities. This has led to a somewhat complicated hypothesis to suggest that surviving Celtic custom caused a widespread shared (or divided) use of one complex by two families or two owners. An infinitely simpler explanation is that in the Roman world a gentleman of any consequence travelled with a considerable retinue of servants and friends, and that visiting one another's country houses was part of the regular social round. For journeys, the reputation of inns was so evil that anyone with the right connections preferred to travel by moving from one acquaintance's villa to another. Most Romano-British villas seem to have been connected by a drive or lane to a public road and the majority were within ten miles or so of a town. Their social relationships to the towns, and perhaps even more to one another, are therefore likely to have been as important as their economic effects.

How much the development of the large villas changed the agricultural scene we do not know. As early as the second century an occasional pattern of villa and village has been observed which seems not unlike that of manor house and village in later ages. It may be that in fourth-century Britain there were comparatively few Diocletianic *coloni* – or that changes in the law made little difference to a situation that had long existed in this relatively undisturbed region of the empire. Small, native-style farms are still much in the majority, though there are some signs of consolidation into larger units. A greater change was the encouragement given to the various trades that served the decoration of the great houses. The best-known of these are the regional 'schools' of mosaicists – firms or groups of firms with workshops centred respectively on Cirencester, Chesterton (Water Newton), Dorchester (Dorset), Brough-on-Humber, and somewhere centrally in the south. Other trades, working in more perishable materials, perhaps operated in similar fashion – for example fresco-painters (of whose work just enough survives to demonstrate its importance and the quality it could reach); furniture-makers; and other suppliers of major items for the well-to-do household.

The ancient countryside was not exclusively agricultural – nor only for the pleasure of the rich. The falling-off of long-distance trade in the third century had given encouragement to more than one British industry, for example the vast potteries of the Nene Valley. In the fourth century we can observe how a similarly huge ceramic industry in Hampshire which had also expanded in the third century – mostly within the area of the later royal forest of Alice Holt – now captured the London market and flourished greatly.

Government and Administration

In these early years of the Late Roman period the principal features of the administrative system had emerged into which the new-style provincial governors fitted. Ultimate decisions might emanate from Milan (which emperors had for some time found more convenient than Rome) or, after 324, Constantinople. But from the time of Constantius I, the central government was for routine purposes situated at Trier, on the Moselle. The head of the civil administration as far as Britain was concerned was the praetorian prefect of the Gauls, based in Trier, to whom the *vicarius* of the British diocese was responsible. The prefecture

Map 2. The provinces of Roman Britain

grouped together Britain, Spain, and northern and southern Gaul. The headquarters of the British *vicarius* was almost certainly in London. Under him were four provincial governors – of Maxima Caesariensis (also probably based in London), Britannia Prima (Cirencester), Flavia Caesariensis (York?), and Britannia Secunda (Lincoln?), each with his own staff. As well as normal civil duties, this structure had a vital military role in being in charge of supply, including the new state factories (a weaving-mill of the sort that supplied the Late Roman army with material for uniforms is, for example, recorded in Britain). A fifth-century document, showing unusual insignia for the *vicarius* of the Britons, may denote that by that time at least he had, exceptionally, some troops under his command. More important is the fact that with supply in civilian hands there was some potential check on the army. Socially the senior members of this new administration were drawn from the educated middle and upper part of Roman society. The British vicariate could be an important stage in a fully professional career, and the men in the post of whom we know were not mediocrities. Into the beginning of the fifth century it remained policy not to employ men in their own provinces in senior posts, and most would expect to serve at some stage at the imperial court.

The financial administration of the provinces was very different from that in the Early Empire. Though the financial headquarters was again in London, the old provincial procurators had disappeared. The governors of the individual British provinces were responsible to the *vicarius* for the taxation in kind which the municipal councils were expected to raise from the individual taxpayer. Independent of the *vicarius*, however, were two other separate financial departments each with a diocesan chief officer, eventually responsible directly to the imperial secretariat. One handled taxation in cash, controlled the issue of coinage, and administered mines and certain other operations. The other was responsible for crown property throughout Britain, and to it reported the local procurators who acted as agents in charge. These two branches, however, often worked closely together and could call on the assistance of provincial governors to carry out their functions in the field.

Military Command

The command structure for the army no longer had to correspond with provinces. At the same time the old distinction between legions and auxiliaries was replaced by a new one categorizing units into garrison, or frontier, troops (*limitanei*) and new, mobile field forces (*comitatenses*), the latter having higher status and remuneration. Many of the old units retained their identity, especially in Britain, where much of the old frontier remained substantially unchanged even if the internal character of units altered. At this time, the units stationed in Britain were classified as *limitanei*, emphasizing its character as a region to be defended rather than a place from which a field army might rapidly be deployed. The commander of a garrison army was entitled *dux* – the *dux Britanniarum* being one such. Mobile forces, on the other hand, tended to be led by a *comes rei militaris*, of superior rank. Under Constantine himself there was only one central field army. But under his warring sons several major field armies emerged, under generals of even higher rank. Certain of these army groups achieved permanence; and smaller task forces drawn from them became operative under such *comites rei militaris*.

The field armies contained both old units that had been retained or reformed and many new ones. Among the latter, an important proportion was raised from peoples of Germanic origin; and in the fourth century there were also many individual German recruits. Something like a quarter of the regular army in the West was German, including the officer corps. In 367 the *dux Britanniarum* defeated by barbarians, for example, was named Fullofaudes. By the end of the century, German generals were occupying the very highest commands. Though it was no longer fashionable for such men to adopt wholly Roman names, they fully absorbed the attitudes and ambitions of their native-born Roman equals. However, as a group the fourth-century army officers tended to be noticeably different, culturally, from their counterparts of equivalent rank in the civil service. Important cultural prejudices, not to say dislike and contempt, appeared between certain emperors and their officers on the one hand and leading civilians on the other; and stresses between emperors, their courts, and their new capitals, and the old aristocracy that still looked towards Rome became socially and politically important.

The Rise of Christianity

The final element in the Constantinian equation was the Church. The traditional public religion of the Roman State had sufficed for public purposes, but offered little to the individual. The breakdown of the Antonine peace and the crises of the third century coincided with a

7. Grand mosaic from a villa of the early fourth century at Hinton St Mary, Dorset, with a central roundel containing a beardless figure generally identified as one of the earliest representations of Christ

widespread desire for a more personal religion that offered consolation and meaning in this world and a better life in the next. Concomitantly, close contact with the East brought about the spread of various Eastern 'mystery religions' offering mystic revelation and personal contact with a deity. Hadrian himself had worshipped at the ancient shrine of the Eleusinian mysteries in Greece and a variety of mystery religions became respectable and accepted. The Persian cult of Mithras gained a powerful hold in military and commercial circles, where its insistence on high standards of probity and discipline and its tightly bound brotherhood matched the ideals and interests of businessmen and officers. Unlike Christianity it was not politically suspect, and therefore not persecuted. In Britain, its chapels appear exclusively where the army or trading community was strong – at Rudchester, Carrawburgh, or Housesteads on Hadrian's Wall, and in London. Its weakness was its very exclusivity, closed to women and largely restricted to one social class. Its rites were sufficiently close to those of Christianity to make them appear blasphemous, and there are possible signs in London and at Carrawburgh, for example, of Christian attack during the Christian ascendancy, and it largely faded away during the fourth century.

Recent work on the survival of Roman Christianity in Britain after the end of Roman rule has suggested that it was more widespread and deeply rooted than was formerly thought. It is important, however, not to read too much back from the fifth and sixth centuries into the third and fourth. It is generally agreed that Christianity had little hold in Britain before the fourth century. Third-century Britain had, indeed, its martyrs – St Alban at Verulamium, SS Julius and Aaron probably at Caerleon. The fact that Britain fell in the part of the empire ruled by Constantius I, whose former wife was St Helena, mother of Constantine, and who permitted the last great persecution to go no further in his area than the demolition of churches, may have had the negative effect of preventing a substantial early martyr cult in Britain. On the other hand, it may also have encouraged well-to-do Christians to transfer their residences from more dangerous parts of the empire, unobtrusively increasing the villa-dwelling population.

Britain has produced the earliest set of church plate yet known from the Roman Empire (from Water Newton), almost certainly very early fourth century in date, while British bishops appear only a year after the 'Edict of Milan' legalized the Church, bearing titles indicating as their sees the capitals of the four British provinces. These facts draw our attention to the fundamental change that came with Constantine the Great. The growth of absolutism in the third century had been accompanied by sporadic imperial attempts to introduce a monotheistic state religion. From the time of Constantine the central new factor in Roman politics (and increasingly in the private sphere as well) was ideology. It was no longer sufficient to observe the customary formalities of the state religion to demonstrate loyalty: Christianity, as the new state religion, required belief. Toleration of pagan practices lasted a long time. But it was gradually withdrawn, despite intense opposition during the whole of the fourth century from a powerful section of the Roman aristocracy, who both saw the old religion as central to Rome herself and identified with it in opposition to the court. There were even to be short periods when there were pagan emperors again, sympathetic to them. Within the Church itself, however, there was a further development of immense significance for its future when the Emperor Constantius II decided that it was an imperial duty to ensure unity on doctrine. From the middle of the fourth century the hunting of heresy by the State added a new dimension to the politics of loyalty.

What must, therefore, surprise us in Britain is not that recent research has indicated a considerable amount of Christianization in the fourth century, but that there is not more. This will lead us to examine the apparent nature of the British church. The old notion of urban Christianity and rural paganism certainly cannot be sustained. Urban communities under Constantine are suggested by the bishops mentioned. A very small possible church excavated inside the walls at

Silchester, and probable examples of the much more common cemetery churches over the graves of martyrs and other prominent Christians at Verulamium, Canterbury, and elsewhere, all point in the same direction. But the grand monuments of fourth-century Romano-British Christianity are associated with the villas: mosaics at Frampton and Hinton St Mary, for example, or the wall-paintings of Lullingstone. The distribution of archaeological evidence suggests that the incidence of Christianity was very patchy. A cemetery at Dorchester in Dorset indicates a large and wealthy Christian community, supported by the surrounding villas; elsewhere similar cemeteries have nothing. A remarkable series of lead baptismal fonts has not come from cities but rural locations or small settlements, likely to have been under the eye of the landowning gentry, and a very substantial proportion of them has been found in East Anglia, where there is evidence of real personal wealth in the Late Roman period.

Constantine had dealt a massive blow both to the pagan cults and to the municipalities by distributing the endowments and treasures of the temples to the Church and by diverting funds from the civic treasuries. Wealth in the fourth century increasingly fell into the hands of the greater landowners on the one hand, and of the State and its institutions on the other. In Britain, where the villas are such an outstanding feature of the period, it is not surprising to find them in the forefront of the development of Christianity. Nor, under these circumstances, is it surprising to find the evidence so patchy. If the strength of Christianity in a district depended on whether or not the local landowner was an enthusiastic Christian (or politically ambitious), then this is exactly what we might predict. If the erection of churches and other Christian monuments had depended on an energetic town council, as had the provision of public temples and other civic amenities in earlier periods, then the provision might have been relatively more even. It is clear that substantially more bishops from Britain were present at the Council of Rimini in 359, but no titles survive and it is therefore not known whether they were city-based. It is perhaps significant that some, at least, were known to have had difficulty in raising the money to pay their travelling expenses.

If, then, the urban Christian communities were weak – or declined over the century after an initial Constantinian boost – what does this imply for the survival of Christianity after the end of Roman rule? The clue is perhaps the eventual reconciliation to Christianity of the landowning class as a whole elsewhere in the West, if this was paralleled in fifth-century Britain. In that period, quite unlike the fourth century, we ought to see a fairly uniform spread of Christianity among the rural population. Since most of the population had, anyhow, always lived on the land, that ought to lead us to expect the general persistence of Christianity, at least as a subculture. Indeed, the fact that in Late Roman times the rural clergy, unlike their urban counterparts, were relatively poorly educated and socially obscure (in the country, even bishops could be little more than dependants of landowners) may have assisted their identification with the agricultural multitude and ensured the survival of a Church as well as a faith, whatever eventually happened to the landed proprietors themselves.

After Constantine

How long did the villa-based society of the fourth century retain its brilliant early prosperity, so different from so many other parts of the empire? Describing a series of raids by barbarians on places near the frontiers of Britain in AD 360, the well-informed contemporary historian Ammianus tells us that at that time 'a pall of fear lay over the provinces' and adds, significantly, that they 'were already exhausted by the accumulation of disaster over the years'. The opinion, moreover, has been advanced, based on the archaeology of the towns, that the latter were 'finished' by about 350 (an opinion which we shall have to interpret later). Details apart, however, the picture is startlingly different from the earlier years of the century.

There is good reason to think that the 'golden age' did not long outlive Constantine himself. His death in 337 left the empire uneasily divided between three sons, Constantius II, Constans, and Constantine II. Britain came within the dominions of the younger Constantine. Dissatisfied with his share, he attacked Constans in 340 and suffered total defeat. It was a long time since the army of Britain had been involved in a military disaster. Subsequent weakness – and possibly disaffection – are probably reflected in a most unusual and unexpected journey across the winter Channel by Constans in person in 343, the brief surviving references to which hint at pressures on the northern frontier. Border problems were certainly acute by 360, the moment to which our quotation from Ammianus refers, when Scots from Ireland and Picts from Scotland had broken an agreement with Rome, implying that there had been earlier threats settled by diplomacy (and probably, in the usual style, with gold). In 364 they were back time and time again, now accompanied by 'Attacotti', probably also from Ireland, and by Saxons. The great barbarian invasion of 367, to which we shall come, was therefore the culmination of a long period of trouble from outside. But events at least as bad had occurred inside the territory under Roman rule.

In 350 a palace conspiracy ended in the murder of Constans and the elevation of an officer of Germanic descent named Magnentius. The Western part of the empire was now at war with the East, under the surviving son Constantius II. The three-and-a-half-year rule of Magnentius, Christian but tolerant of pagans, proved disastrous in its consequences. Constantius II, whom we have already seen assuming the duty of suppressing Christian heresies, also hated paganism – indeed he reintroduced the death penalty for its observance and scandalized the senate by removing the ancient Altar of Victory from the Senate House in Rome. With his final victory, Britain came under special scrutiny. The appointment of the head of the imperial establishment records office, one Paulus, was made with the aim of hunting down dissidents in the island. Black humour aptly nicknamed him 'The Chain'. His brief was to arrest certain military men who had supported Magnentius, but he soon extended this, unchecked, into a reign of terror in which false evidence played a dominant part, horrifying even the most loyal officers. Constantius' own *vicarius* of Britain, Martinus, sacrificed himself in a brave but unsuccessful attempt to put an end to Paulus. One cannot but suspect that many leading families which had been implicated in incidents in the past half-century were drawn into this whirlpool, in addition to those involved in current politics. Confiscations, exile, imprisonment, torture, and executions were approved by the emperor without any questioning of the evidence. The confiscations of property alone must have had a profound effect on the landed prosperity of Britain, while the devastation of morale among both civilians and army can only have left them in a weaker state to resist the barbarian troubles now pressing in on them.

Barbarian Incursions

The nadir came in 367. Picts, Scots, and Attacotti invaded Britain; Franks and Saxons attacked the coast of Gaul. Both the central imperial command – the Emperor Valentinian himself was in northern Gaul – and the senior officers responsible for Britain were taken by surprise. The *dux* in command of the static garrison of Britain was put out of action and the *comes* in charge of coastal defence killed. The most remarkable feature was the concerted action of such disparate barbarians. Treachery by native frontier scouts in the north is one attested part of the situation, but to account for the total operation we have to suppose an unknown barbarian with extraordinary military and diplomatic ability. Detailed knowledge of Roman dispositions and understanding of Roman military methods were not hard to come by, with so many Germans in the Roman army (though conscious disloyalty to Rome is very rarely indeed to be suspected). What convinces one of inspired barbarian leadership is the fact of simultaneous attacks by peoples with very different cultures, from homelands relatively distant from one another, with a very clever division of targets – and, perhaps most of all, with the maintenance of complete secrecy. The Romans certainly called it a conspiracy, and it is difficult not to agree with them.

Once in Britain, the barbarians ranged unchecked in small bands, looting, destroying, taking prisoners, or killing at will. The countryside near to roads must have been particularly vulnerable and not all walled towns seem to have resisted. Both civil authority and military discipline broke down. Troops deserted, some claiming – unconvincingly – to be on leave. Political opportunists seized their chances. Britain was being used as a place of dignified exile for high-ranking offenders, and one well-documented conspiracy among them was nipped in the bud just after the Roman recovery of Britain. But there is also some evidence that one of the provinces of the British diocese (which had now been divided into five, rather than four) fell temporarily into the hands of rebels.

The response of Valentinian to the calamity was the dispatch of a small but powerful task force of elite troops under a *comes rei militaris*, Theodosius, who was the father of the later emperor Theodosius the Great. Such task forces became a frequent method of dealing with emergencies under the Late Empire: Britain had already been the scene of such an expedition (in 360), possibly more than once. At this time these forces were usually made up of *comitatenses*. From the end of the fourth century, barbarian war bands under their own kings, even whole tribes, became more and more often accepted into Roman armies. Task forces thereafter tended to be made up of a mixture of whatever regular troops could be found and barbarian allies, or sometimes barbarians alone on contract for a specific campaign or operation. Looking forward, it is important to realize that in the fifth century, as military practice evolved out of that of the fourth century, 'the barbarians' were not like some hostile aliens from outer space but were a familiar fact of life. Barbarian warriors were frequently employed against other barbarians in the suppression of internal disorder, and for the prosecution of Roman civil wars.

Theodosius' conduct of the campaign and subsequent reconstruction of Britain seem to have been both brilliant and thorough. London was spectacularly relieved. Garrison troops were reassembled, deserters pardoned, and an effective army re-created. The barbarian war parties on land were picked off one by one and the Saxons defeated at sea. Goods stolen from the provincials were recovered and returned. Civil authority was restored under a new *vicarius*; the province that had been lost to rebels was regained and named Valentia in honour of Valentinian and his eastern colleague and brother, Valens. Forts were rebuilt and damaged cities restored.

Reconstruction and Renewal

The extensive remodelling of town defences in Britain by the addition of prominent external towers, dated archaeologically to somewhere in the middle of the fourth century, is perhaps more convincingly to be attributed to Theodosius' initiative than to any other, although the variety in design and arrangement does suggest that, once again, the cost and responsibility fell on the local councillors. However, the fact that it is always the full circuit that was retained in use has very important implications for the state of the towns in the middle and late fourth century. Such wide circuits cannot have been kept solely to provide military strong points or even as refuges in time of danger for a dispersed rural population. There was something worthwhile defending with permanent works. What, then, are we to make of the notion that the towns of Britain were 'finished' by about 350? The unspoken assumption that fourth-century towns were of the same sort as those of the second is clearly mistaken. We have, of course, to be careful not to assume that all towns changed in the same ways. Yet the decay or disuse of civic public buildings is hardly surprising in the context of municipal treasuries raided by central government and councils made up of now unwilling members. Fourth-century legislation repeatedly tried to prevent members of the class that now had the hereditary obligation to serve from moving their main residences away from the

61

towns, while those in higher social classes were exempt from municipal obligations. The new element in society was the vastly expanded bureaucracy, and it is in their direction that we should probably be looking. Five governors, their staffs, households, companies of guards, and the many others connected with them needed housing; and there were numerous other officials with inflated establishments and lifestyles supported by substantial allowances. At each level in the hierarchies, expectations existed which in the end filtered down from the lavish grandeur of the Late Roman court. Large areas of fourth-century capitals such as Trier or Arles, once normal municipalities, were given over to palaces and other associated official buildings. On a smaller scale, we ought to expect such a pattern in many towns in Britain. In fact, archaeology has demonstrated the building of large town houses in places as different as London and Carmarthen, and urban development into the middle of the fifth century at Verulamium and, of a distinctive sort, at Wroxeter. In the cultivated open spaces of this period observed within the city walls in excavations we should perhaps

8. Late Roman defence: town wall of Caerwent, Gwent, with external towers added in the fourth century

see the gardens and grounds of the new-style establishment rather than a decay represented by abandoned building sites. Indeed, in London and York at least we may reasonably expect the presence of emperors themselves from time to time to have made a mark on the archaeological record.

There is no reason to think that the Theodosian restoration was other than outstandingly successful. Archaeologically, it is clear that many villas continued in occupation; some were enlarged and others built from scratch. Hadrian's Wall was occupied to the end of Roman rule, even if individual garrisons were smaller than before. A new system of signal stations was established on the north-east coast. Much industry had been interrupted by the war of 367, but the many changes in pattern after it indicate vigour and new initiatives. Not surprisingly, some pagan religious sites disappear, but others continue in cult use, while still others show signs of conversion to new uses, some perhaps Christian, towards the end of the century. The forty years from 369 do not have the brilliance of the early fourth century, but the island does not provide any evidence for the sort of despair that the historians report for the 50s and 60s. In order to understand what happened in 409 it is important to realize that in the last part of the fourth century Roman Britain had not been running rapidly downhill.

This period is, in fact, marked by two more occasions on which major attempts on the imperial throne were launched from a base in Britain. In 382 a victory over the Picts by a general named Magnus Maximus (Macsen Wledig in Welsh legend) created for him a reputation that led to proclamation as emperor and the rule, for five years, of the part of the empire represented by the Gallic prefecture – Britain, Gaul, and Spain. In Britain, some forts, notably in the Pennines and Wales, were abandoned at this time and the Twentieth legion was withdrawn from Chester, but it remains still entirely uncertain whether Maximus' campaigns and eventual defeat at the hands of the Emperor Theodosius the Great had any significant overall effect on the defensive capability of the army in Britain. Between 392 and 394 Britain was peripherally involved in another palace revolt for the duration of which Theodosius lost control of the Western empire, but the significance of this incident lies more in the appearance of a general, a Frank in this case, overshadowing a compliant emperor in the West. The death of Theodosius in 395 made this new balance of power in the Western imperial government the rule, rather than the exception, for the rest of its history. The joint accession of Theodosius' sons, Honorius in the West and Arcadius in the East, inaugurated a period in which the pattern of government in the two halves of the empire diverged fundamentally. In the East, it remained firmly in the hands of the emperor, or his chief civilian minister. In the West a powerful landed aristocracy, rooted in its estates, vied for influence with the professional soldiers who commanded the armies. After three-quarters of a century, both these parties were to come to the conclusion that they could manage without an emperor in the West.

Chapter 4
The End of Roman Rule

The effective control of the West by the late Emperor Theodosius' chief lieutenant, Flavius Stilicho, son of a Vandal officer in the Roman army and a Roman mother, was accompanied by a claim to the East as well. Plot, counterplot, and civil war between Stilicho, Honorius, the Western senate and the Goths under Alaric did much to ensure in the long term the collapse of Roman rule throughout the West. In Britain, initial successes against Picts, Scots, and Saxons, and restoration of defences under Stilicho's direction were probably followed at the very beginning of the fifth century by some posting elsewhere of troops. We do not know the extent of the postings, but the cessation of bulk import of new coinage in 402 must mean that neither remaining regular troops nor civil officials were henceforth paid from central sources. It is not surprising that we find a mood of extreme discontent. In 406 the army in Britain elevated the first in a rapid succession of three emperors. On the last day of that year, large numbers of barbarians crossed the Rhine. The central government withdrew the administration of the prefecture of the Gauls to Arles, and had no time to deal with usurpers in Britain.

The third usurper ran true to form, seizing Gaul and Spain, and for some while was recognized as a legitimate colleague by the unwilling Honorius. Once again, we do not know if there was an overall reduction in the garrison of Britain, but some further withdrawal of regular units seems likely. The north-western empire of Constantine III, however, was to be the last of its kind, and before it was finally extinguished Britain had ceased for ever to be under any sort of imperial rule.

We know tantalizingly little about the process by which this happened, but something can be pieced together. In 408 the absence of the bulk of Constantine's army in Spain left him unable to deal with heavy barbarian attacks on Britain. In 409 the mutiny of that army under its British-born commander (and his deliberate incitement of the barbarians in Gaul) coincided with renewed assaults on Britain by enemies who included Saxons. At this point, Britain itself – along with parts of Gaul – rebelled, expelling Constantine's administration. Britain successfully took on the barbarian invaders, and henceforth broke decisively with Roman rule.

How Britain expelled the invaders and what was then the state of the country can only be the subject of informed speculation. There are slight hints that Stilicho and Honorius had taken some steps to encourage local organization of, or payment for, defence. It is most unlikely that the regular army was retained when Constantine's officers were deposed, or that the elaborate administrative structure which supported it was manned and paid. Under the Late Empire, the landed class strongly resisted both the conscription of the agricultural labour force into the regular army and the payment of taxes. Elsewhere in the fifth century units whose pay stopped disbanded and dispersed or settled on the land. Indeed, from AD 455 the final running-down of the Western regular army seems to have been in progress. In Britain, with no central government, it is all the more likely that in the years from 409 groups of barbarians were paid to undertake the fighting, and some of these may already have been brought in under Constantine III or even Stilicho.

There is no sound reason for thinking that the Britons elevated any more emperors, or re-created any of the mechanisms of central government. Not only had very few of them had experience of senior office (unlike recent Gallo-Romans), but – if they shared the sentiments of the landed class elsewhere in the fifth-century West – they are most unlikely to have wanted to reassume the burdens of supporting the system of imperial administration once they had been rid of it. The critical success of the Flavian governors of Britain in the first century had been to convince the native aristocracy that its advantage lay with Rome. There is no good reason to think that the events of 409 had destroyed the position of the landowning class. They are, however, very likely indeed by now to have lost confidence in the system of emperor, bureaucracy, and army as the best way of securing their still prosperous way of life. They will not have been encouraged by the ruthless political persecution in Gaul by Honorius' officers after the fall of Constantine III.

The presence of a full paper establishment of military and civil posts for Britain in a Late Roman document known as the *Notitia Dignitatum* suggests that into the fifth century it was assumed centrally in the imperial ministries that Britain would be recovered – as it had so often been in the past. There was, in fact, only one short period, from 425 to 429, when a Roman military intervention in Britain was again a serious possibility. But by that time other groups of well-to-do Roman provincials, particularly in a large area of Gaul, were starting to settle down tolerably comfortably, employing, in alliance with, or under the rule of, barbarians.

Provided that the barbarians remained amenable, any of these arrangements might suit the gentry better than direct imperial rule. But for the weakened middle and artisan classes, who in the fourth century had depended more and more on the army, civil service, and urban church for jobs, patronage, or markets, the change must have been disastrous. In Britain, the Roman archaeology supports such a picture. Early in the fifth century, the massive pottery industry comes to an apparently abrupt end; by 420–30 coinage ceases to be in regular use. These facts, incidentally, make the dating of the end of the occupation of Roman sites in the fifth century much more difficult than in earlier periods. There is, however, certainly no evidence for villas having come generally to a violent end. Signs of how late towns might be active vary a good deal. At Lincoln we find a main street being resurfaced well into the fifth century; in London imported Mediterranean pottery in the ash of the heating system of one house combines with other evidence to suggest normal occupation in the early fifth century; the forum at Cirencester was being kept up after the cessation of general circulation of coins; and at Verulamium a sequence of important buildings succeeding one another on the same site is closed, strikingly, by the laying of a new water-main at a time that cannot be far short of the middle of the century.

After the break with Rome the Britons, we are told, lived under *tyranni*, or 'usurpers', best interpreted as local potentates who had filled the vacuum left by the removal of legitimate authority. Their background was probably very varied, some perhaps landowners, others military men, Roman or barbarian, who had been invited to take control or seized power. At Gloucester, a rich warrior burial with equipment apparently from the eastern part of the Roman world may possibly represent a *tyrannus*, or a *condottiere* in local pay. At Wroxeter, ambitious fifth-century timber buildings may well represent the headquarters of such a leader.

In 429 St Germanus, a prominent Gallo-Roman bishop who moved in high Roman circles, visited Britain to combat heresy, debating publicly with British magnates at Verulamium 'conspicuous for their riches, brilliant in dress, and surrounded by a fawning multitude'. The visit to Britain he repeated around 446/7, though apparently in deteriorating circumstances. At least until the 440s, therefore, something survived in Britain that was very like 'post-Roman' or 'post-imperial' life elsewhere in the West.

Further Reading

Before the Roman Conquest

R. Bradley, *Social Foundations of Prehistoric Britain* (Harlow, 1984), subtle analysis.

B. Cunliffe, *Iron Age Britain* (London, 1995), general account of the centuries immediately before the Roman Conquest.

B. Cunliffe, *Greeks, Romans and Barbarians* (London, 1998), how Gaul and Britain were drawn into the Graeco-Roman world.

S. James, *The Atlantic Celts: Ancient People or Modern Invention?* (London, 1999), controversial and important.

General Surveys

P. A. Clayton (ed.), *A Companion to Roman Britain* (Oxford, 1980), exceptionally well-illustrated essays.

P. Dixon, *Barbarian Europe (The Making of the Past)* (Oxford, 1976), excellent, well-illustrated background reading, helping to place the end of Roman Britain in its European context.

S. Frere, *Britannia: A History of Roman Britain* (3rd edn, London, 1987), a standard work.

B. Jones and D. Mattingley, *An Atlas of Roman Britain* (Oxford, 1990).

M. Millett, *The Romanization of Britain* (Cambridge, 1990), a specifically archaeological approach.

Ordnance Survey, *Map of Roman Britain* (4th edn, Southampton, 1978), two sheets (scale 1:625,000) and gazetteer.

P. Salway, *Roman Britain* (*Oxford History of England*, vol. Ia) (Oxford, 1981), large-scale general history with essays on major themes.

P. Salway, *The Oxford Illustrated History of Roman Britain* (Oxford, 1993).

M. Todd, *Roman Britain 55 BC–AD 400: The Province beyond Ocean* (Fontana History of England) (London, 1981), perceptive narrative.

R. J. A. Wilson, *A Guide to the Roman Remains in Britain* (3rd edn, London, 1988), recommended to those wishing to visit the accessible material remains of the period.

Special Aspects

A. Birley, *The People of Roman Britain* (London, 1979), illuminating study based on the people known by name in Roman Britain.

D. J. Breeze, *Roman Scotland* (London, 1996), current thought on the northern frontier.

M. Henig, *The Art of Roman Britain* (London 1995).

M. Henig, *Religion in Roman Britain* (London, 1984).

P. A. Holder, *The Roman Army in Britain* (London, 1982), welcome first modern account.

R. Merrifield, *The Archaeology of Ritual and Magic* (London, 1987), includes much illuminating reinterpretation of Romano-British material.

A. L. F. Rivet and C. Smith, *The Place-Names of Roman Britain* (London, 1979), major work of reference: gazetteer, accompanied by linguistic and geographical analysis.

C. Thomas, *Christianity in Britain to AD 500* (London, 1981), thought-provoking re-examination.

Chronology

Entries in **bold** denote events belonging to the general history of the Roman Empire.

71–84	Conquest of Wales and north completed
	Conquest of Scotland
	Trajan (98–117)
c.100	Scotland temporarily lost: frontier on Tyne–Solway line
	Hadrian (117–38)
122	Hadrian in Britain: the Wall begun
	Antonine Emperors (138–92)
	Antoninus Pius (138–61)
140–3	Antonine advance into Scotland: by 143 Antonine Wall begun
c.158	Serious trouble in northern Britain
c.160	Temporary reoccupation of Antonine Wall
	Marcus Aurelius (161–90); major wars on the Danube
c.163	Hadrian's Wall restored
193	Clodius Albinus proclaimed in Britain
	Severan Emperors (193–235)
197/213	Britain becomes two provinces
208–11	Campaigns of Septimius Severus and Caracalla in Scotland
235–70	**Imperial crisis: civil wars and invasions in East and West**
260–74	**'Gallic Empire'**
270s	Renewed growth in Britain
	Diocletian (284–305)
	'The Tetrarchy'
287–96	Carausius and Allectus
296	Britain recovered by Constantius
after 296	Britain becomes civil diocese of four provinces
	House of Constantius (305–63)
306	Campaign of Constantius I in Scotland; Constantine the Great proclaimed at York
324	**Constantine sole emperor; foundation of Constantinople**
340–69	Period of severe stress: internal troubles, harrassment by barbarians
350	**Magnentius proclaimed in Gaul**
353	**Constantius II sole emperor**

Index

Page numbers in *italics* refer to illustrations or captions. There may also be textual references on the same page.

Expand your collection of
VERY SHORT INTRODUCTIONS

Visit the
VERY SHORT
INTRODUCTIONS
Web site

www.oup.co.uk/vsi

➤ **Information** about all published titles

➤ News of **forthcoming books**

➤ **Extracts** from the books, including titles
not yet published

➤ **Reviews** and views

➤ **Links** to other **web sites** and main
OUP web page

➤ Information about **VSIs in translation**

➤ **Contact** the editors

➤ **Order** other **VSIs** on-line

VERY SHORT INTRODUCTIONS

Derived from the best-selling *Oxford Illustrated History of Britain*, the following British history titles are now available in the Very Short Introductions series:

➤ **Roman Britain**
Peter Salway

➤ **The Anglo-Saxon Age**
John Blair

➤ **Medieval Britain**
John Gillingham & Ralph A. Griffiths

➤ **The Tudors**
John Guy

➤ **Stuart Britain**
John Morrill

➤ **Eighteenth-Century Britain**
Paul Langford

➤ **Nineteenth-Century Britain**
Christopher Harvie & H. C. G. Matthew

➤ **Twentieth-Century Britain**
Kenneth Morgan

ARCHAEOLOGY
A Very Short Introduction
Paul Bahn

This entertaining Very Short Introduction reflects the enduring popularity of archaeology – a subject which appeals as a pastime, career, and academic discipline, encompasses the whole globe, and surveys 2.5 million years. From deserts to jungles, from deep caves to mountain tops, from pebble tools to satellite photographs, from excavation to abstract theory, archaeology interacts with nearly every other discipline in its attempts to reconstruct the past.

'very lively indeed and remarkably perceptive … a quite brilliant and level-headed look at the curious world of archaeology'

Barry Cunliffe, University of Oxford

'It is often said that well-written books are rare in archaeology, but this is a model of good writing for a general audience. The book is full of jokes, but its serious message – that archaeology can be a rich and fascinating subject – it gets across with more panache than any other book I know.'

Simon Denison, editor of *British Archaeology*

www.oup.co.uk/vsi/archaeology

HISTORY
A Very Short Introduction
John H. Arnold

History: A Very Short Introduction is a stimulating essay about how we understand the past. The book explores various questions provoked by our understanding of history, and examines how these questions have been answered in the past. Using examples of how historians work, the book shares the sense of excitement at discovering not only the past, but also ourselves.

'A stimulating and provocative introduction to one of collective humanity's most important quests – understanding the past and its relation to the present. A vivid mix of telling examples and clear cut analysis.'

David Lowenthal, University College London

'This is an extremely engaging book, lively, enthusiastic and highly readable, which presents some of the fundamental problems of historical writing in a lucid and accessible manner. As an invitation to the study of history it should be difficult to resist.'

Peter Burke, Emmanuel College, Cambridge

www.oup.co.uk/vsi/history